香港國際詩歌之夜 2013
INTERNATIONAL POETRY NIGHTS IN HONG KONG

編輯 Editors

北島 Bei Dao

陳嘉恩 Shelby K. Y. Chan

方梓勳 Gilbert C. F. Fong

柯夏智 Lucas Klein

馬德松 Christopher Mattison

颯雅・林恩

Zeyar Lynn

目錄 Contents

1 Breaking News

Not an unusual afternoon to enjoy an idle slothfulness.
The world, however, has to revolve as it can't do otherwise.
Spinning confusedly, it generates stop press news every 30 seconds.
If the media like it, it flashes on global screens.
And here comes … the darling of world media,
Kim Jung Il is dead.
Much beloved and cherished by the revolutionary masses,
The Great Leader, Kim Jung Il
Is dead.
The absolute dictator of North Korean nuclear-capability,
At 69, the lover of wine and women, is dead.
"Constantly striving to improve the people's lives,"
Kim Jung Il is dead.
Whilst he was traveling by train, with the people's welfare on his mind,
His heart stopped beating. And so … Kim Jung Il is dead.

The whole world—including China, Japan, America, and South Korea—
Is in a fix.
Crowds line the streets and make a clamor of their condolences.
Generals salute with copious tears.
The Great Leader Kim Jung Il is (finally) dead.

Just the other day, Vaclav Havel passed away.
Champion of democracy, leader of the Velvet Revolution, Mr. Vaclav Havel,
Builder of a new state based on justice, dramatist Mr. Havel,
Who petitioned a military regime to release a woman held under house arrest.

If you could go to both funerals,
Which one would you attend?
The world's dignitaries graced Havel's funeral.
As for Kim Jung Il's,

The whole country was ordered to appear, to cry their hearts out
At the funeral. Each and every citizen.
A rumor floated that stone-throwing would be allowed at the funeral.
Provided that details of the type of stone, size, weight, and motive are given
Accurately in advance, the authorities will consider it deeply.

Stones are not rare in any part of the world.
Stones have not been rare in the world since the Stone Age.
Stones covered with blood.

突發新聞

一個沒什麼特別的下午享受閒散。
但世界，卻必須旋轉彷彿此外別無選擇。
在困惑中旋轉，每30秒產生一條新聞。
碰到媒體喜歡的，就會閃動在世界各地的屏幕上。
現在是……全世界媒體的寵兒，
金正日死了。
被革命群眾愛戴和崇敬的
偉大領袖，金正日，
死了。
北韓核力量的唯一獨裁者，
69歲，紅酒和女人的熱愛者，死了。
「持續努力改善人民生活」，
金正日死了。
當他正乘火車出行，心裏記掛著人民的幸福，
他的心臟停止了跳動。那麼……金正日死了。
全世界——包括中國、日本、美國和南韓——
面臨修整。
人們列隊上街，喧嘩弔唁。
上將敬禮，滿噙淚水。
偉大領袖金正日（終於）死了。

就在另一天，瓦茨拉夫·哈維爾去世。
民主的捍衛者，天鵝絨革命的領袖，瓦茨拉夫·哈維爾先生，
一個以正義為根基的新國家的建立者，劇作家哈維爾先生，
請願軍政府釋放一個被軟禁在家的女人。

如果你可以去兩個葬禮，
你會去哪一個？
全球政要為哈維爾的葬禮增光添彩。
至於金正日的葬禮，
整個國家的人民都被命令出現，在葬禮上
嘔心痛哭。每一位公民都要。
一個謠言流傳開去，説葬禮上允許人投擲石頭。
只要提前準確告知石塊的種類、大小、重量、動機等細節，
專家們會審慎考慮。

石頭在世界任何地方都不少見。

石頭在這世界上自石器時代起就不少見。
沾滿血的石頭。

（曹疏影譯）

2 I Am Silence

I look coldly at your hullabaloo
From the top of the abyss. Below, I see your rampant destruction.
Your steel objects flashing in sunlight. Sparks off the anvil,
Texts, flags and pennants, enormous myths,
Like a desert snake whose stomach is stitched up zig-zag,
Sounds of hooves, diseases, lusts,
Compilations of indescribable victories.

Not getting what you wanted, you laid waste to everything in your way.
Fragments of words, slithered syllables, dried and twisted bones of
Consonants, stains of vowels.

Dare to touch me, your hands will sizzle.
I am Silence.
The poison darts in your heart are my couriers.
All invisible frozen shadows belong to my language.

I am always here.
Come and search for me with your swarming
multitudes.
I am here. I am always here.
I am Silence.

我即靜默

我從深淵之頂
冷眼看你的喧囂。向下，我看見你猖獗的毀滅。
你的鋼器在日光下閃耀。鐵砧上火花迸濺，
文本，旗幟和三角旗，龐然神話，
如沙漠中的蛇，它的胃被蜿蜒縫合，
來自蹄、疾病、色欲的聲響，
難以描摹的勝利彙編一處。

沒得到你想要的，你把擋著你的一切毀滅掉。
字詞的碎片，滑動的音節，乾而扭曲的
輔音的骨頭，元音的污漬。

敢來觸碰我，你的手會嘶嘶作響。
我即靜默。
你心中的毒飛鏢是我的快遞。
所有隱形、冷凍了的陰影都屬於我的語言。
我一直在這裏。
來用你雲集的大多數搜尋我。
我在這裏。我一直在這裏。
我即靜默。

（曹疏影譯）

3 My Heart Beating on a Plate

Such bliss! My Lord is shining his gun barrel
While I'm on all fours,
Licking clean his boots.
With gratitude, I lick both sides simultaneously.

My Lord appreciates industriousness. Shining his barrel,
He occupies the land. Makes two kings war against each other.
In a minion state, orders munitions factories to be built,
And breeds his clones.

I am loyal to my Lord. He got me as a bonus at the slave market.
My Lord is my universe. He had me
Scalped and left to dry in the sun. A splash of water, then, again,
Left to dry out.
My brains are properly cooked and tender.

My Lord approaches the window and whistles.
A child runs out of the camp. My Lord never misses. Straight
In the middle of the forehead. Before my gums have growled,
The target practice is dragged away.

My Lord goes into the bedroom. A newly-musked woman at the ready.
He closes the door. Signals the end of my day. Must be the allergy
In my blood. I stare up to the moon
And howl.

Sitting on my bamboo bedstead, undressing, I peel off my skin,
Unlock each bone from its joint and place them neatly in a row.
From a hole in the wall
I slide out.

I am free as long as my Lord is asleep. The lawn outside
is freezing.
A dark forest. A hushed village. I enter a hut and go to
the back,
Where I kneel down and wash my face
With water from an earthen bowl.

我的心在盤子裏跳動

如此福佑！當我四肢伏地，
他正擦亮他的槍筒
我舔淨主人的靴子。
帶著感謝，我同時舔著兩邊。

我的主人欣賞我的勤奮。擦亮他的槍筒，
他佔領土地。令兩個國王互戰。
在其領地上，號令建造軍需品工廠，
繁殖他的克隆人。

我忠誠於我的主人。他在奴隸市場找到我，算是撿
　　到了。
我的主人是我的一切。他剝了
我的頭皮，在太陽下晾乾。用水潑濕，然後，再次，
晾乾。
我的大腦於是又熟又嫩了。

我的主人走近窗子吹響口哨。
一個孩子從帳篷裏跑出來。我的主人絕不錯過。直
　　接
在那額頭的正中。在我牙床發出低嘯之前，

練習目標已被拖走了。

我的上帝走進臥室，一個剛薰好麝香的女人已準備
好。
他關上門。這標誌著我的一天結束了。一定是我的
血
出現過敏。我向上盯著月亮
嚎叫。

坐在我的竹床架上，寬衣，我脫下我的皮膚，
把每一塊骨自其關節拆卸下來，整齊擺放好。
從牆上一個洞裏，
我滑走了。

只要主人睡著，我便擁有自由。外面的草地在結霜。
暗黑的森林。寂靜的村莊。我走進一間茅舍，走進
最裏面，
我跪下，洗臉
用陶碗裏盛著的水。

（曹疏影譯）

4 My Own Voice

In this world of physical and mental samsara strung on a thread
I am a gaseous compound, a hybrid species, a sponge.
From the holes in my being I peek at the mosaic called the Outer World.
He who turned his back on me left me in a tangle.

Has he jumped into a war refinery to become a new weapon?
Will he be missing me like the howl of a skin-and-bone dog
Left in the memory of a home deserted by refugees?
Has he become a chipped stone to be used as a piece of chalk
To be written on the wall of new myth, or embedded in the 5-month-old
Foetus discarded from a biomedical lab?

Oh … sweet human. Oh … poor lamb.
Into which kaleidoscopic pattern has he been rotated?

I have tried to hammer my little voice into a brick wall
The voice that only he knows to be his own
Amid roars and growls, explosions and earthquakes,
shrieks of pain,
I'm not even half a vowel. I flow from him, and this
flow
Deliberately tortures me into sound.
Is this alien sound resounding in me heralding
imminent disaster?
A bell with no sounding rod in it once clanged
throughout this world
Before disappearing from the face of the earth,
For the majority of mankind who merely lived and
merely died.

Tying all the fissures, erasures, cuts into a knot
I try to sound my incurable voice to the highest pitch.
In my own voice, of course. I tried to call him, the
owner of my voice.
I spat out the sound that came out clearly from my
mouth.

That's not my voice. That's their voice forced into my
mouth.
My own voice has gone dumb and hoarse and broken
The distance between my own voice and him is
serpentine.

Will the lost one bear the same name as the one written
on a bomb
Dropped over fellow citizens? Will he be the industrial
nail of capitalist
Slavery hammered into the cracks
Of an agriculture-based economic dream?
A blindly loyal needle threading the dictator's coat
With the blood of everyone?
Will that poor one be living it up, like a fish packed in
salt?

我自己的聲音

在這身體、心靈之輪迴纏於一線的世界裏
我是一個氣態化合物，雜交物種，一塊海綿。
從自我存在的孔洞中，我偷看那被稱為「外部世
　　界」的馬賽克。
那背對著我的人，把我留在糾繞之中。

他是否已跳入戰爭的熔爐，變成一件新武器？
他會否思念我，如一頭皮包骨的瘦狗
被遺在難民棄土的記憶中？
他是否已變做一塊破碎的石頭，被人當作粉筆，
在新神話的牆上寫字，或插進那從生物醫學實驗室
　　裏
扔出來的、五個月的胚胎身上？

噢，甜美的人類。哦，可憐的羔羊，
旋轉著被捲入哪一個的千變萬化的花紋？

我試著將我細小的聲音捶打進一道磚牆
只有他自己知道那是自己的聲音，那聲音
在怒吼和咆哮，爆炸和地震，痛苦的尖叫之中
我甚至不是半個元音。我從他流過，這流動

故意折磨我成為聲響。
這在我裏面迴響著的陌生的聲音，是否預示災難將
　　至？
鈴鐺沒有鈴芯，但它的叮噹聲曾響過這個世界
在它從地球面前消失之前
為那大多數僅僅是活過、死了的人類。

紮上所有的裂痕、抹去和清除的東西，打成結
我試著把我無可治癒的聲音拉到最高。
用我自己的聲音，當然。我試著叫他，我聲音的主
　　人。
我從嘴裏清晰地吐出聲音。
那不是我的聲音。那是他們強行塞到我嘴裏的聲
　　音。
我自己的聲音已經嘶啞破碎
我自己的聲音和他之間的距離是蜿蜒的。

那迷失者的名字，是否與擲向同胞的炸彈上
寫著的名字相同？他是否將成為資本家奴隸制的
一顆工業釘，被敲入以農業為基礎的
經濟大夢的裂隙之中？

一根盲目忠誠的針，用每個人的鮮血
縫製獨裁者的大衣？
那可憐的人兒是否將過快活的日子，如同用鹽醃製
的魚？

（曹疏影譯）

5 Not So Oblivious to the Surroundings

After Constantine Cavafy: 1863–1933

Can't we ever depart from this city, Cavafy?
You were right. Whichever city I visit, I'm back in this
  same city.
Even if I were in a foreign city I've never been to,
On foreign roads I've never taken,
I would see the same road, the same buildings, the
  same
Dead traffic lights, the same potholes, the same
  vehicles, the same envies,
The same ignorance, the same sounds, the same battles,
  the same ways of life
The same wealth, the same huge billboards, the same …
Between cars going and to and fro, I see you crossing
  the street towards me
Ancient Mariner just off *Odyssey*'s ship after the long
  voyage and the long war.
Smelling of the sea, the blood of heroes, sex, myth,
  mixed with all that, this city,
(Let me say it) and Poetry.
Atop this mountain is my white pagoda and the sounds

of small bells attached
There on that mountain is your, what do you call it …
temple?
The great hall where you worship your gods.
Delphi, on Mount Parnassus, says, "Know Thyself."
I have not known myself for a long time now, Cavafy.
In the daily confusion of living and struggling, I, too,
roll and reel.
Here, they are laying down the foundations of what
you Athenians started,
Demos kratia, the new gods with their data, their
feelings and emotions,
Their meta-narratives, and the truth that issues forth
from the barrel of fixed
Heavy artillery. My whole life has been a longing for
Socrates' hemlock!
Old issues have become new issues.
Can't I escape from this city, Cavafy?
International debt now strangles the Greeks. Senior
citizens with pension cuts.

Civil servants with salary cuts. Workers made redundant
due to recession.
Riots on the streets, security forces in the same boat
with the rioters.
Bullet-proof gear, dark shades, whistles, shields,
truncheons, tear gas,
Versus anger, sorrow, escape from suffering.
Fellow sufferers, those brainwashed by power, and
others crushed
Under walls of power.
Modern multinational gods in skyscraper penthouses,
Look down on the commotion below with glasses in
their hands:
People, like tiny particles, coming together in a rush,
breaking up helter skelter,
Re-grouping in clusters.
Clouds of smoke cover up the scene and then slowly
disperse.
As if it were ritual. And the gods watch this, their
conversations intact

On top of Olympus, Zeus and his cohorts,
Down below, tiny Sisyphusses.
Zeus threatens to hurl his thunderbolt of law and order.
Arab Spring in the world. Culture-clash.
"Nationalism." "Progress." "Whose benefit?"
Wherever I go, I'm back in the same place. As you said, "Even if you die,
You will die in this place." That was in 1932. This is 2012, Cavafy,
And the world is going to end 21/12/2012. We already have Hitler, Gaddafi,
Bertolt Brecht, Yannis Ritsos, and Tiananmen Square. We meet them again
Here in this city. In the streets of the Base and the Superstructure,
On the beaches of Structuralism and Post-structuralism,
At the horizon of the sea of interpretations,
As I stand knee-deep in the crashing waves,

I know I am back here in the city centre.
Battleships gleaming in the port load fresh sacrificial
offerings
For war's forthcoming banquets. Chemical weapons.
Cluster bombs.
Touchbutton gadgets. Advancements. Concealments.
Abuse of power
And resultant destructions. New expectations. From a
city-state to new States.
Cities imposing religious teachings …
Conclusions. Continuations.
Energizing speeches, victory gongs, blood brothers,
Evermore manipulated are people, masses, citizens …
This city is winding up my invisible spring again,
Cavafy.
Troy is calling out to me again.
I hear the neighs of the inescapable Trojan Horse.
Is this the only city left
In the whole global village, Cavafy?

並非無視周圍的一切

仿康斯坦丁・卡瓦菲斯(1863–1933)

卡瓦菲斯，難道我們真的不能離開這座城市？
你是對的。無論我去哪裏，我都是回到同一座城
　　市。
即使我在一個從未去過的外國城市，
走在從未走過的陌生道路上，
我總是看見同一條路，一樣的樓房，一樣的
壞掉的交通燈，路上一模一樣的坑窪，一樣的汽
　　車，一樣的妒忌，
一樣的無知，一樣的聲音，一樣的戰鬥，一樣的生
　　活方式
一樣的財富，一樣的巨型廣告牌，一模一樣的……
車流穿梭間，我看見你穿過馬路向我走來，
遠古的水手剛剛走下《奧德賽》的船隻，他們已經
　　歷了漫長的旅程和漫長的戰爭。
海水的味道，英雄之血，性，神話，什麼混在一
　　起，這座城市，
（且容我說出）和詩歌。
在這山頂的，是我的白塔，它的小鈴鐺作響
在那山上的，是你的——你叫它什麼來著——廟
　　宇？

那裏宏偉的殿堂是你膜拜你的神靈的地方。
德爾斐，在帕納賽斯山上，說：「認識你自己」。
如今，我已很久不認識自己了，卡瓦菲斯。
生活和掙扎每日給我困惑，我也在其間碌碌轉轉。
在此地，他們正放下你們雅典人奠下的基石，
民主，新的神靈帶著他們的數據、感覺和情緒，
他們的元敍事，和從修整好的重型大砲中提取出的
真理。我全部生命都在渴望著蘇格拉底喝下了劇毒
的鐵杉！
舊議題變做新議題。
難道我不能逃離這座城市，卡瓦菲斯？
國際欠債正在勒死希臘人。長者的養老金在削減。
公務員被減薪。經濟衰退令工人賦閒。
街上在暴亂，保安部隊和暴徒在同一條船上。
防彈裝置，暗影，呼哨聲，盾牌，警棍，催淚瓦
斯，
而另一邊是憤怒，悲傷，免除苦痛的逃亡。
同是受難的人群，一些被權力洗腦，另一些在權力
之牆下
被擊碎。

摩天大廈頂層公寓中的現代跨國神靈，
俯視著騷動，把眼鏡握在手中：
人們，如細小的粒子，急促聚集，又忙亂分開，
重組成群。
煙霧雲層覆蓋了這些景象，又緩慢消散。
彷彿這是一場儀式，神靈注視這些，他們對話完整
在奧林匹斯山上，宙斯和他的同伴們，
在下面，是小小的科林斯王們。
宙斯發出威脅令，投下他法律與秩序的雷電。
這世界的阿拉伯之春。文化衝突。
「民族主義」。「進步」。「誰的利益？」
無論我去哪裏，我都在會回來同一處地方。就像你
　　說的，「即使你死，
也是死在這裏。」那是在1932年。而這裏是2012
　　年，卡瓦菲斯，
世界就要在2012年12月21日抵達末日。我們已經
　　有了希特勒、卡扎菲、
布萊希特、揚尼斯·里索斯和天安門廣場。在這座
　　城市
我們再次遇上他們。在基礎和上層建築的街道上，

在結構主義與後結構主義的沙灘上，
在詮釋的海平線上，
當我站立，雙膝浸入拍岸波浪之中，
我知道，我又回到了這座城市的中心。
港口閃亮的戰艦，為戰爭即將到來的宴會
裝載著新鮮的祭品。化學武器。集束炸彈。
觸式配件。進步。隱秘。權力的濫用。
和繼之以來的毀壞。新的期待。從一個城市國家，
　　到新城邦。
強制宗教教育的城市……
結論。延續。
充滿活力的言論，勝利的鑼鼓，同宗的弟兄，
永被操控的，仍是人民，大眾，公民……
這座城市正再次結束我那隱形的春天，卡瓦菲斯。
特洛伊再次召喚我。
我聽見無可逃避的特洛伊木馬的嘶鳴。
這是整座地球村
遺留下來的唯一一座城市嗎，卡瓦菲斯？

（曹疏影譯）

6 Oil

Involved one way or the other in oil exploration,
Our costs, production costs, human costs, cultural costs,
Environmental costs—traditional fuel depletes as does tradition.
Between lifestyles and conservation, between energy requirements and
Reasonable price, between fuel for all and domination of technology,
The real value of oil goes missing. Every time a car engine starts,
Every time a pot of rice is cooked, every time the least trivial task is done …

We do not speak to oil.
We do not listen to oil.

Now that it has come to this, whatever shall we do?
They say oil has made a decision about us. With a thousand eyes offshore,
And a dark storm ominously in the corner of the sky.

In which country did
Thakhin Po Hla Gyi, working class hero and leader of the Burmah Oil Company
Oilfield workers' uprising live?
How much is a barrel of human life worth?
An oil tanker flying international flags sails into the dusk with a full belly.
Splits in two somewhere off shore. Belly ripped open. Gigantic waves
Encrusted with oil particles crash against the shore and die en-masse.
They say the sea can no longer be bathed clean.
Shall we go and lick a drop of oil in the night café?
At which stage of the Carbon cycle are you metabolized?
What's heating up isn't just your hair. The poles are melting. Seawater, rising.
It's not just in your neighborhood. How much confiscated oxygen
Goes into the culture of carbon monoxide?
What sort of fuel keeps you alive?

Oil wells are on fire. Even the sky is ablaze.
Oil well fires cannot be extinguished. And neither can the fire in the sky.
You are going to combust.
Your body coated in oil. Your crude oil heart. Your petroleum lips.
Sucking, biting, and kissing your honeymoon.

Oil is simple.
Oil is mystical.

石油

以一種或另一種方式捲入石油開採
我們的成本，生產成本，人力成本，文化成本，
環境成本——傳統燃料如同傳統本身，消耗殆盡。
在生活方式和保育之間，在能源需求
和合理價格之間，在一切能源需求和科技統導之
　　間，
石油的真正價值消失了。每發動一次汽車引擎，
每煮一鍋飯，每完成一次細小、瑣屑的任務……

我們不與石油交談。
我們不對石油傾聽。

於是就成了現在的樣子，我們還能做些什麼？
他們說石油已為我們做好決定。一千雙眼睛離岸，
不祥的風暴已出現在天空一角。是在哪個國家，
緬甸石油公司工人中的英雄和領袖 Thakhin Po Hla
　　Gyi
帶領大家為生存而起義？
人的生命，一桶能值多少錢？
飄揚著國際旗幟的油輪撐著吃飽的肚皮，駛進黃
　　昏。

在離岸的某個地方，拆成兩半。肚皮被撕開。巨浪綴滿石油，猛拍海岸，集體死亡。
他們説大海無法洗淨了。
我們能去夜裏的咖啡館舔一滴石油嗎？
你在碳循環哪一個環節被代謝？
受熱的不止是你的頭髮。兩極熔融。海水高漲。
這事不止發生在你隔壁。有多少被充公的氧
轉為一氧化碳？
哪種燃料讓你還活著？
油井中烈焰燃燒，天空也在閃亮。
油井的火無法熄滅。天空中的火便也不能。
你將燃燒。
你的身體塗上石油。你的原油心。你的石油唇。
吸吮，咬，和親吻著你的蜜月。

石油是簡單的。
石油是神秘的。

（曹疏影譯）

7 The Returnee

After packaging him up neatly,
They sent him back home as a gift.

When the package was opened
Everyone received a fright—
His body was in stitches.

"What on earth happened?"
Some asked with sympathy.
Someone had overdone it. His lips too were stitched.

His eyes were blank.
In the stitches of his memory lay a dark night.

He just stared
At the brightly-colored, beautifully-designed
Packing paper that had wrapped and packaged him,
That made a susurrus sound when touched.

歸來者

他們將他打好一個包，
送回家，像寄送一份禮物。

打開包裹
人人都吃了一驚——
他的身體是縫起來的。

「究竟發生了什麼？」
一些人同情地問。
一些人反應過度。他的唇也是縫著的。

眼中只有空白。
他記憶的針腳裏，躺著一個黑夜。

他只是盯著
那用來包裹他的包裝紙
色澤明亮，設計精美
碰一碰就會悉窣響。

（曹疏影、朱曉玢譯）

8 Whale

To let in some fresh air, I open the window.
On the street lies a dead blue whale.
People and vehicles move into / over / under / in front /
on the left / on the right of the dead whale. Traffic flows
As usual, unimpeded. No one sees the dead whale.
It's invisible, as air.

To let in some fresh air, I open the window.
On the road are the usual scenes: streets, platforms, trees, buildings,
People, cars. And sounds of engines, voices. All according to the script.
I open the door, but it won't budge. I apply some pressure and
Through the doorway, I see the white belly of a blue whale.
And what seems like a beating heart, swelling and shrinking under its skin.

News spreads that municipal workers have got rid of the dead whale;

City dwellers can now carry on with their daily lives in
peace.

To let in some fresh air, I open the window. What's that
Stench coming into the room? Something dead
between the roof and the
Ceiling? Under the bed? In my hair? Behind the
cupboard? Hear that?
The heart beat beat beat beat beat beating? The whale?
No,
It's coming from your heart (on the left side of your
chest)
Like suffering from some urban psychological disorder,
A delusion of instinct.

And now, the phone rings.
One hand goes straight into the dead whale's mouth.
"Hello, it's me. I'm still lying on the road."

鯨魚

為了透一透氣，我打開窗。
街上，躺著一頭死去的藍鯨。
人和車子，趟過、碾過、穿過它，在它面前、
左面和右面繞過它。交通如常，
順暢通行。沒有人看見這頭死去的鯨魚。
它是隱身的，如同空氣。

為了透一透氣，我打開窗。
路上，什麼都和平日一樣：街道、站台、樹，樓房
人，和車。發動機的聲音，人聲。一切照常。
我去開門，但推不動。我用了用力
來到門口，看見一頭藍鯨的白肚皮
和那像是跳動的心臟在，在皮膚下膨脹，收縮。

新聞說市政工人已將死鯨清理掉了，
市民勿需擔心，可以照常過日子

為了透一透氣，我打開窗。撲面而來的惡臭
是怎麼回事？什麼東西死在屋頂和天花板之間了
　　麼？

死在床下？我的頭髮裏？櫥櫃後面？聽到嗎？
那心臟跳跳跳跳跳一直跳？鯨魚？不，
這聲音是你的心跳（在你胸口的左邊）
像是患上了城市的某種心理失序，
一種本能的妄想。

現在，電話響了。
一隻手探入死鯨嘴裏。
「你好，是我。我還躺在路上。」

（曹疏影、朱曉玢譯）

颯雅．林恩，緬甸現代詩人，已出版七本詩集、兩本國際詩人詩作翻譯選本（包括中文詩）、五本譯詩集（西爾維亞．普拉斯、日本現代詩選、日本短歌集、約翰．阿斯伯里，以及查爾斯．伯恩斯坦），以及三本詩論與詩學文集。他還將緬甸文譯為英文。

在緬甸詩歌界，林恩積極介紹蘇聯後俄語詩歌、紐約派、語言派(L=A=N=G=U=A=G=E)寫作、Flarf詩歌運動，以及泛稱為「後現代」的詩歌，因而響出名堂。

林恩在仰光首辦聯合國教科文組織「世界詩歌日」，現在該活動已在緬甸廣為人知。

在緬甸，林恩打破主流的「現代」（緬甸文為Khit Por）詩而享負盛名。他開創了一個新的詩歌方向，偏重建構而非表達，偏重理智而非抒情。同時，他一直關注社會政治事件。他於2004年發表「後現代(Post-Khitpor)宣言」，啟發年輕一代去發掘一條正統和主流詩歌模式之外的新路徑。「現代」(Khit Por)詩歌仍是主流，「當代詩」卻已成為「另類」詩歌。

林恩曾參加2012年倫敦國際詩歌節。其詩作英譯本收錄於《骨將鳴：緬甸當代詩人十五人》。

他現居於仰光，在一所私立學校中教授英語，並編輯緬甸詩歌三季刊《詩世界》。

Zeyar Lynn, a contemporary Myanmar poet, has already published seven collections of poetry, two anthologies of miscellaneous poetry translations of internationally acclaimed poets including Chinese, five translations of poems (Sylvia Plath, modern Japanese poetry, Japanese tanka, John Ashbery, and Charles Bernstein), and three books of collected articles on poetry and poetics. He also translates from Myanmar to English.

He is known for having introduced post-Soviet Russian poetry, the New York School of poetry, L=A=N=G=U=A=G=E Poetry, Flarf, and what is generally termed "postmodern" poetry into Myanmar.

He was also the first to organize the UNESCO World Poetry Day event in Yangon, which has now become popular throughout the country.

He has earned a reputation in Myanmar for having broken against the mainstream "Khit Por" (Myanmar for "modern") poetry and set out a different path that is recognizably constructivist rather than expressionist, cerebral rather than emotional, while at the same time not losing sight of the political events in society. His *Post-Khitpor Manifesto* (2004) opened the way for the younger generation to look for a way out of the dominant and mainstream poetic model. While Khit Por is still mainstream, contemporary poetry has now become its alternative, or "Other."

He participated in the 2012 London Parnassus International Poetry Festival. His poems have appeared in English in *Bones Will Crow: 15 Contemporary Burmese Poets*.

Currently, he lives in Yangon where he teaches English in a private school and also works as an editor of the tri-quarterly Myanmar poetry magazine called *Poetry World*.

出版 Publisher
香港中文大學出版社 The Chinese University Press

封面影像 Cover Image
北島 Bei Dao

出版日期 Date of Publication
二零一三年十一月 November 2013

國際書號 ISBN
978-962-996-617-1

香港國際詩歌之夜 2013 International Poetry Nights in Hong Kong 2013
主辦單位 Organizers
香港中文大學文學院 Faculty of Arts, The Chinese University of Hong Kong
香港浸會大學文學院 Faculty of Arts, Hong Kong Baptist University
香港科技大學人文社會科學學院 School of Humanities and Social Science, The Hong Kong University of Science and Technology

合作夥伴 In Partnership With
英國文化協會 British Council

協辦單位 Co-organizers
時刻文化 Moment Communications
香港中文大學出版社 The Chinese University Press

贊助 Sponsors
香港兆基創意書院 HKICC Lee Shau Kee School of Creativity
中國會 The China Club
周凱旋基金會 Chau Hoi Shuen Foundation

Printed in Hong Kong